# Covered Wagons

## Hands-on Projects About America's Westward Expansion

### Jennifer Quasha

The Rosen Publishing Group's
PowerKids Press™
New York

**Some of the projects in this book were designed for a child to do together with an adult.**

*For Sue, who also headed west for a new life*

Published in 2001 by The Rosen Publishing Group, Inc.
29 East 21st Street, New York, NY 10010

Copyright 2001 by The Rosen Publishing Group, Inc.

First Edition
Book Design: Felicity Erwin

Layout: Michael de Guzman

Photo Credits: p. 4 © North Wind Picture Archives; pp. 6–21 by Pablo Maldonado.

Quasha, Jennifer.
    Covered wagons : hands-on projects about America's westward expansion / Jennifer Quasha.— 1st ed.
        p. cm.— (Great social studies projects)
    Includes index.
    Summary: Briefly discusses American westward expansion in the 1800s, with related projects and activities, such as making a small covered wagon, flatboat house, trail journal, and lantern.
    ISBN 0-8239-5704-7 (alk.paper)
    1.West (U.S.)—History—To 1848—Study and teaching—Activity programs—Juvenile literature. 2. Overland journeys to the Pacific—Study and teaching—Activity programs—Juvenile literature. 3. Frontier and pioneer life—West (U.S.)—Study and teaching—Activity programs—Juvenile literature. 4. Pioneers—West (U.S.)—History—Study and teaching—Activity programs—Juvenile literature. 5. Pioneers—West (U.S.)—Social life and customs—Study and teaching—Activity programs—Juvenile literature. [1.Frontier and pioneer life—West (U.S.) 2. Handicraft.] I. Title.

F592 .Q37 2001
978'.02—dc21                                                        00-029855

Manufactured in the United States of America

# Contents

1  Westward Expansion                          5

2  Covered Wagon Model                         6

3  Flatboat House Model                        8

4  Twine Trail Journal                        10

5  Log Cabin Model                            12

6  Wooden Pioneer Ax                          14

7  Native American Paper Tepee                16

8  Tin Can Lantern                            18

9  Cardboard Fiddle                           20

10 How to Use Your Projects                   22

   Glossary                                   23

   Index                                      24

   Web Sites                                  24

# Westward Expansion

Between 1760 and 1850, American **pioneers** made new paths across the country. Many of the pioneers traveled west in covered wagons. At first people went as far as the Mississippi River. They **settled** on the land alongside the river. When that area became too crowded, pioneers went farther and farther west in search of open land. Eventually people reached the West Coast and the edge of the Pacific Ocean. Dreams of a new life, adventure, and lots of land to farm were exciting, but being a pioneer wasn't easy. The trails were tough to travel on and the weather could be either freezing cold or boiling hot. The pioneers had to live off the land and keep warm, dry, and healthy during long, hard trips.

*Pioneer families had to carry food, supplies, and belongings in their covered wagons. The wagons were almost like houses on wheels.*

# Covered Wagon Model

Most of the covered wagons the pioneers traveled in were about 10 to 12 feet (3 to 3.7 m) long. These wagons could carry up to 2,500 pounds (1,100 kg). The wagon's cover was made out of **canvas**. Sometimes women and children rode inside the wagon. Sometimes they walked alongside it because it was crowded and uncomfortable to ride inside. The trip west took about four months. Here's how to make a covered wagon model:

**tools and materials**

- piece of cardboard, 8 1/2″ x 11″ (22 x 28 cm)
- scissors
- sheet of white paper
- top of cardboard box (shoebox or smaller)
- masking tape
- four brass tacks
- paint
- paintbrush
- two pieces of yarn, 8″ each (20 cm)
- two small plastic horses

6

Cut four circles out of the cardboard. Each circle should be 3 1/2" (1.9 cm) across. Cut a piece of white paper, lengthwise so it is the right size to fit inside the box top. Poke a hole with the scissors at each end of the box top's long side. Now poke a hole in the center of each cardboard wheel.

 Tape the white paper in an arched shape to the box top. Place a brass tack into the center hole in each wheel, then into the side of the box top.

Paint the wagon and let it dry.

 Use the yarn to tie the horses to the wagon. (Often travelers used oxen instead of horses.)

# Flatboat House Model

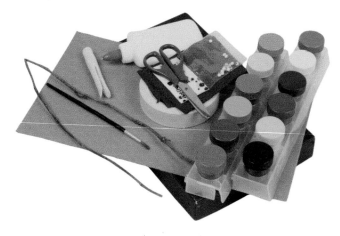

Some pioneers went west by floating on the Ohio River in a flatboat instead of traveling in wagons over land. A flatboat is a large, flat raft with a house built on top. The pioneers needed the house to protect themselves and their belongings against harsh weather. Often a few families would share a flatboat to save money. Here's how to make your own flatboat house model:

**tools and materials**

- piece of cardboard, 16" x 8" (41 x 20 cm)
- scissors
- masking tape
- paint
- paintbrush
- clothespin
- red felt
- white glue
- googly eyes
- two twigs
- black shoe box top

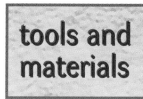

8

Cut out four 2" x 7" (5 x 18 cm) strips from the cardboard. These will be the house walls. Cut out two 4" x 8" (10 x 20 cm) cardboard rectangles for the roof.

 Tape the sides of the house together with masking tape. Tape the two rectangles together to make the roof.

 Paint the flatboat house. Paint the clothespin to look like a person. Let dry. Add red felt for arms. Glue on googly eyes.

 Cut two small holes in the roof of the house for the "legs" of the clothespin to fit into. Glue twigs to the clothespin to make poles for steering the flatboat. Use black shoe box top for raft.

# Twine Trail Journal

Most pioneers traveled west on trails. There were a few main trails leading west, including the Oregon Trail and the Santa Fe Trail. These trails started in Independence, Missouri. Many pioneers, both children and adults, kept journals. These trail journals are now important historical **documents** that tell us how difficult life was on the journey west. Here's how to make your own journal:

**tools and materials**

- scissors
- hole punch
- two pieces of cardboard, 5"x 8" (13 x 20 cm)
- 20 pieces of white paper, 5" x 8 " (13 x 20 cm)
- two pieces of twine, 6" each (15 cm)
- black marker

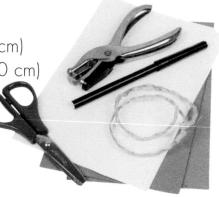

**1** Use scissors or hole punch to make two holes in one of the 5" (13 cm) sides of each piece of cardboard. Punch the holes about an inch (2.5 cm) away from the edge of the cardboard.

**2** Stack the pieces of white paper together. Put the paper between the two pieces of cardboard, lining them up. Punch two holes in the white paper in the same place where the holes are in the cardboard.

**3** Thread a piece of twine through one of the holes in the front piece of cardboard, the paper, and the back piece of cardboard. Do the same with the other hole. Tie each piece of twine in a knot.

**4** Write the words "My Journal" on the front piece of cardboard (the cover) with black marker, and decorate it.

# Log Cabin Model

Once settlers reached the West, they needed to build homes. The cabins had to be ready before winter. Sometimes the settlers had to build very quickly. These first cabins usually were only one room and were built out of logs from trees. The settlers cut **notches** in both ends of the logs so they would fit together tightly to keep out cold drafts. Glass windows were rare. Often settlers made windows using animal skin or paper instead of glass. Here's how to make your own log cabin:

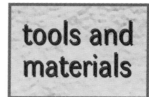

**tools and materials**

- snap-on building sticks
- masking tape
- one sheet of brown construction paper
- scissors

**1** Using four sticks, create a square base for the house. Add sticks until each side of the house is seven sticks high.

**2** Tape together two strips of seven sticks to make both sides of the roof. Tape 16 sticks together, back to front, to make a chimney. Once taped, break off ends of top two sticks. Then break off a smaller piece of next two sticks to give the chimney a narrowing effect.

**3** Tape on roof and chimney.

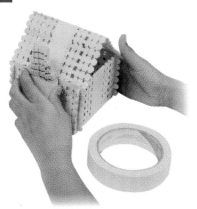

**4** Cut paper windows and doors from brown paper, and tape onto the sides of the house.

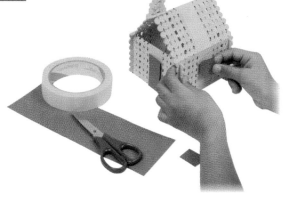

# Wooden Pioneer Ax

Settlers did not have many tools when they first arrived out West. This was because there was only so much space to carry things on their flatboat or covered wagon. However, every settler had an ax. Axes were used for many tasks, including building a house and cutting firewood to keep families warm. Other tools pioneers used included an **auger**, which is a type of tool used for **drilling**, and if they were lucky, a saw. Here's how to make your own pioneer ax:

**tools and materials**

- two 8 1/2" x 14 (22 x 36 cm) pieces of cardboard
- scissors
- wood glue
- balsa wood, 1" x 46" x 1/4" (2.5 x 46 x 0.6 cm)
- aluminum foil

**1** Cut from cardboard the shape of the head of an ax. Cut the same shape from the second piece of cardboard.

 Glue each ax head to one side of balsa wood.

**3** When dry, wrap ax head with aluminum foil.

# Native American Paper Tepee

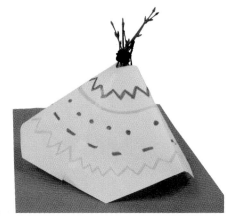

The settlers weren't the only people who lived out West. Native Americans had been living there for hundreds of years before them. The Native Americans of the American Great Plains lived in **tepees**. The frames of the tepees were wood poles covered with buffalo skins. A flap was left open at the top of the tepee so smoke could escape when fires were lit. Tepees were easy to put up and take down so the Native Americans could move easily.

Here's how to make your own tepee:

**tools and materials**

- yarn
- six twigs
- three sheets of white paper
- scissors
- tape
- colored markers

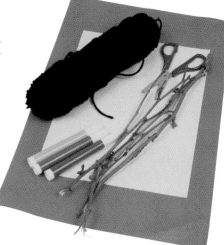

Wrap yarn around the top of six twigs to hold them together. When yarn is tight, spread the sticks out.

 Cut each piece of paper almost in half as shown.

 Tape the sides of the paper together and decorate using markers.

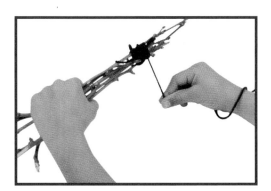

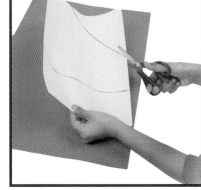

 Tape the paper around the sticks.

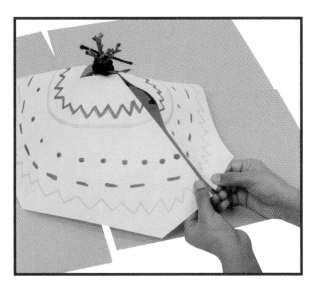

# Tin Can Lantern

Fire and light were very important to the settlers. Fire kept them warm, provided a place to cook their food, and gave them light to see when it became dark. Lanterns were another way the settlers got light. They used a sheet of iron, a hammer, and a tool with a sharp point to make a lantern. The settlers punched holes in the lantern so that it would not only give off light but also look pretty. Candles were made from **tallow**. Here's how to make your own lantern:

**tools and materials**

- masking tape
- empty, clean tin can
  (Can should be smooth, without ridges.)
- black permanent marker
- two heavy books
- bulletin board tack
- small hammer
- paintbrush and black paint
- wire handle
- small candle

**1** Using the masking tape, cover the tin can. Using the black marker, draw a design onto the can.

**2** Place the tin can between two heavy books to hold in place. Hold tack firmly in one hand and hammer holes into the tin can following design. Also make two holes opposite each other at the top of the can for the wire handle.

**3** Take off the masking tape and paint the can black. Let dry.

**4** Place wire handle into the holes at the top of the can to make a handle. Add small candle. (Do not light without adult help.)

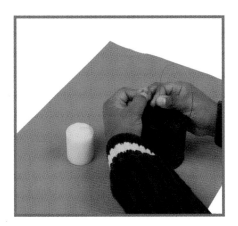

# Cardboard Fiddle

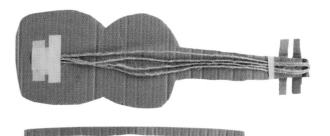

When the settlers had time for fun, they would play games and music. They would also dance. Many people played the fiddle. A fiddle is a string instrument like a violin. It has a bow, which is made out of wood and horse hair covered in **rosin**, or tree sap. The bow is moved across the strings to make various notes. During parties, fiddlers often played their fiddles very fast while others clapped their hands and danced. Here's how to make your own fiddle:

**tools and materials**

- black marker
- brown cardboard
- strong scissors
- twine
- masking tape

With the black marker, draw the outline of a fiddle onto the cardboard. Also draw the handle of the bow.

 Carefully cut out the fiddle and bow. Cut four pieces of 18-inch (46-cm) twine.

 Tape the pieces of twine onto the bottom of fiddle. Loop twine around top and tape other ends to the back.

 Place masking tape lengthwise on the bow.

# How to Use Your Projects

You have learned some important information about America's westward expansion. You have also made some great projects! There are many different things you can do with them. Your projects would make nice gifts or decorations. Brighten up your bedroom with your Native American paper tepee. Your tin can lantern would make a nice homemade holiday gift for a friend or relative. Maybe your log cabin model will come in handy for a school project.

Use and display your projects as reminders of an exciting time of growth and adventure in the history of the United States.

# Glossary

**auger** (AW-ger)  A tool for making holes in wood.

**canvas** (KAN-ves)  A strong cloth with a coarse weave, often made of cotton.

**documents** (dah-kyoo-MENTS)  Written or printed papers that give information and can be used as fact.

**drilling** (DRIH-ling)  The act of making, or boring, holes.

**notches** (NAHCH-ez)  Cuts shaped like a V that are made in the edge of a surface.

**pioneers** (PY-uh-neerz)  Some of the first people to settle in a new area.

**rosin** (RAHZ-in)  Tree sap.

**settled** (SEH-tuld)  To have made your home in a new place.

**tallow** (tah-LOH)  The fat of sheep or cattle after it has been melted. It is used to make candles.

**tepees** (TEE-peez)  Tents used by North American Indians. Tepees are made of hides sewn together and stretched over poles arranged in the shape of a cone.

# Index

**F**
fiddle, 20
fire, 16, 18
flatboat, 8, 14

**L**
lanterns, 18, 22
log cabins, 12, 22

**M**
Mississippi River, 5

**N**
Native Americans, 16, 22

**O**
Ohio River, 8
Oregon Trail, 10

**P**
pioneers, 5, 6, 8, 10, 14

**S**
Santa Fe Trail, 10
settlers, 12, 14, 16, 18, 20

**T**
tepees, 16, 22
tools, 14, 18

# Web Sites

To learn more about America's westward expansion, check out this Web site:

http://tqjunior.thinkquest.org/6400/